THE LORD OF THE RINGS
THE MOTION PICTURE TRILOGY
INSTRUMENTAL SOLOS

Special Thanks to: Paul Broucek, Lindsay J. Harrington,
Robbi Kearns, Mitch Rotter, Lori Silfen, John Walsh

Project Managers: Jeannette DeLisa and Bill Galliford
Art Layout: Martha Ramirez
Music/Arranging Supervisors: Giancarlo Vulcano and Bill Galliford
Arranged by: Tod Edmondson, Ethan Neuburg and Bill Galliford
Engraving Manager: Al Nigro
Engraver: Adrian Alvarez

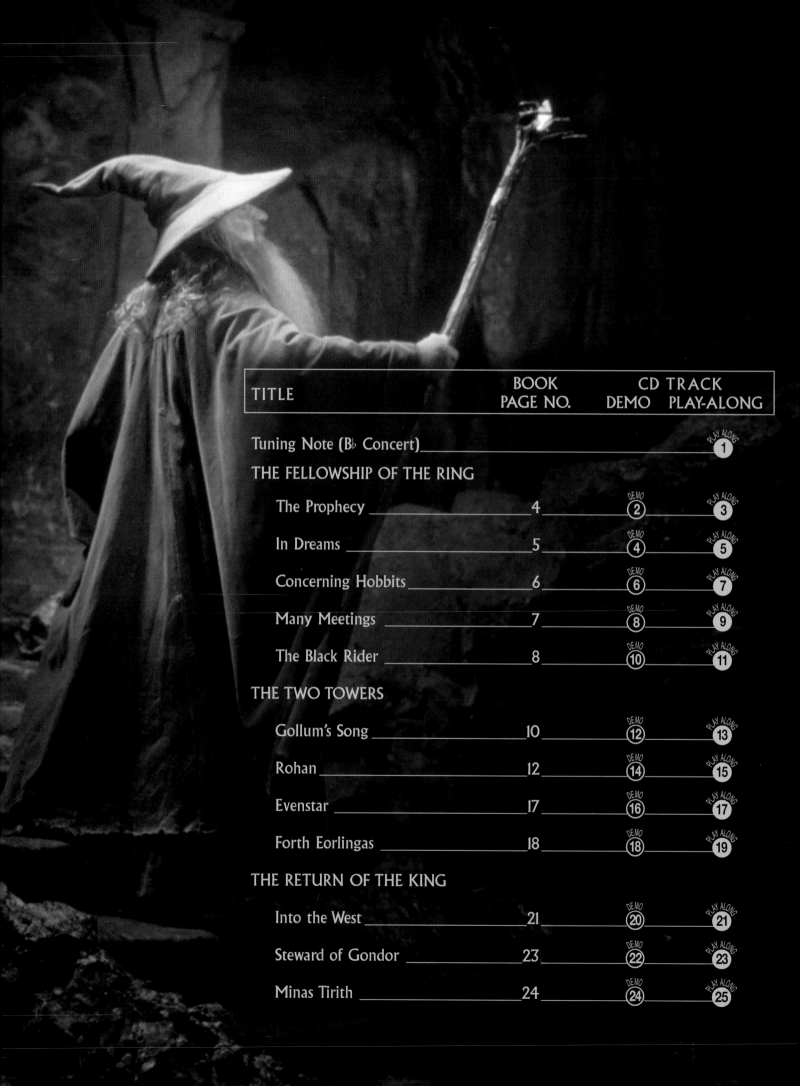

THE PROPHECY

Music by
HOWARD SHORE

IN DREAMS

Words and Music by
FRAN WALSH and
HOWARD SHORE

*C♭ = B♮ **G♭ = F♯

IFM0410CD

CONCERNING HOBBITS

Music by
HOWARD SHORE

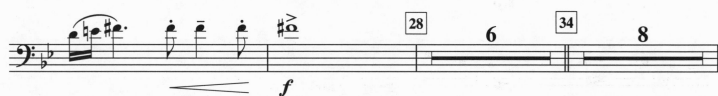

IFM0410CD

MANY MEETINGS

Music by
HOWARD SHORE

THE BLACK RIDER

Music by
HOWARD SHORE

*Gb = F#   **Cb = B♮

IFM0410CD

GOLLUM'S SONG

Words by FRAN WALSH
Music by HOWARD SHORE

Slowly, flowing (♩ = 52)

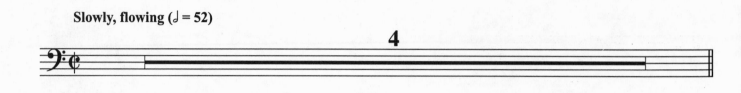

Gollum's Song - 2 - 1
IFM0410CD

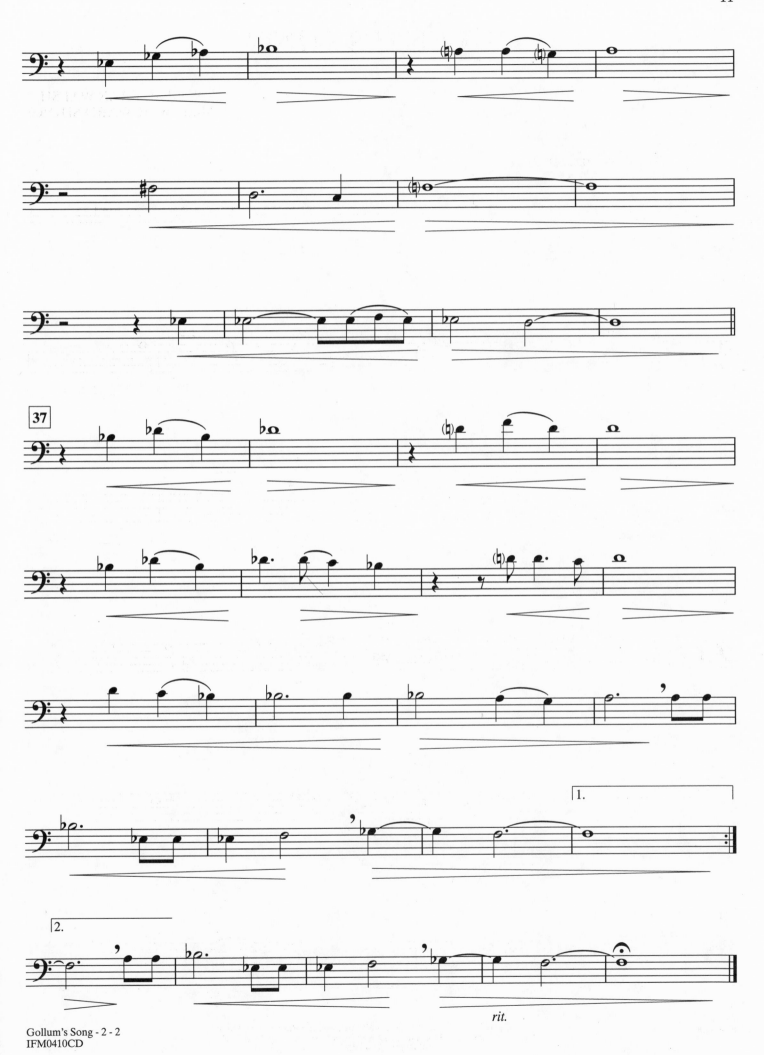

ROHAN

Music by
HOWARD SHORE

EVENSTAR

Music by
HOWARD SHORE

IFM0410CD

FORTH EORLINGAS
(Includes "The March of the Ents")

Music by
HOWARD SHORE

Moderately bright (♩ = 144)

16 **Half as fast (♩ = 72)**

THE MARCH OF THE ENTS
32 **Tempo I (♩ = 72)**

Forth Eorlingas - 2 - 1
IFM0410CD

INTO THE WEST

Words and Music by
HOWARD SHORE, FRAN WALSH,
ANNIE LENNOX

Into the West - 2 - 1
IFM0410CD

THE STEWARD OF GONDOR

Music by
HOWARD SHORE

MINAS TIRITH

Music by
HOWARD SHORE

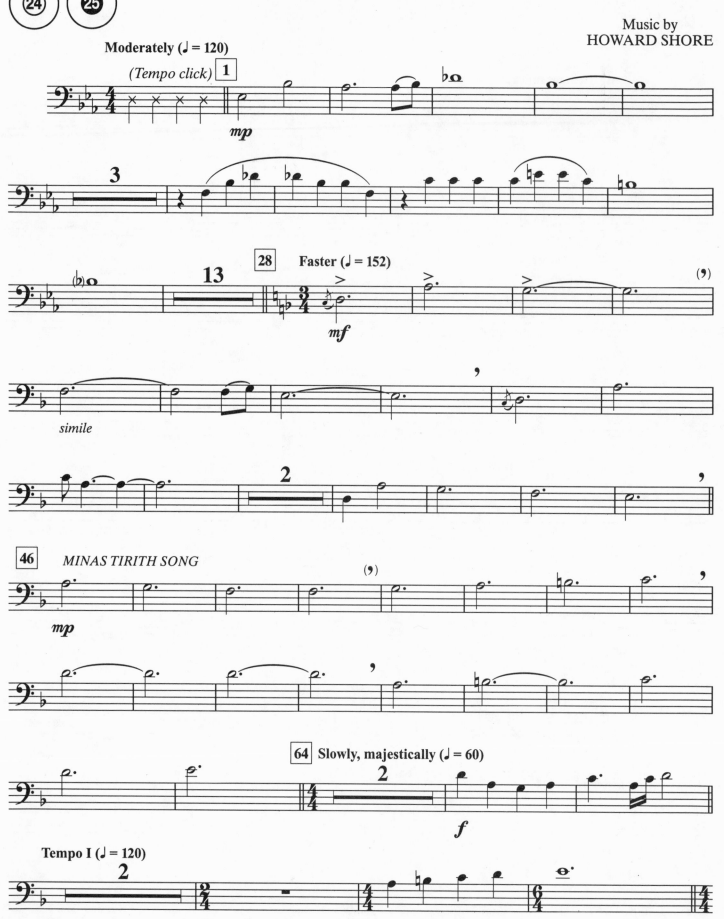

MITRANDIR SONG

PARTS OF A TROMBONE AND POSITION CHART

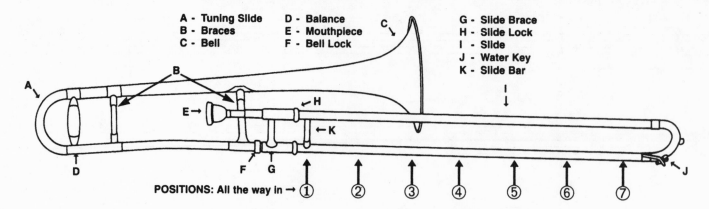

A - Tuning Slide
B - Braces
C - Bell
D - Balance
E - Mouthpiece
F - Bell Lock
G - Slide Brace
H - Slide Lock
I - Slide
J - Water Key
K - Slide Bar

POSITIONS: All the way in → ① ② ③ ④ ⑤ ⑥ ⑦

How To Read The Chart

The number of the position for each note is given in the chart below. See the picture above for the location of the slide bar for each position. When two enharmonic tones are given on the chart (F# and G♭ as an example), they sound the same and are played with the same position. Alternate positions are shown underneath for trombones with a trigger (T=thumb trigger).

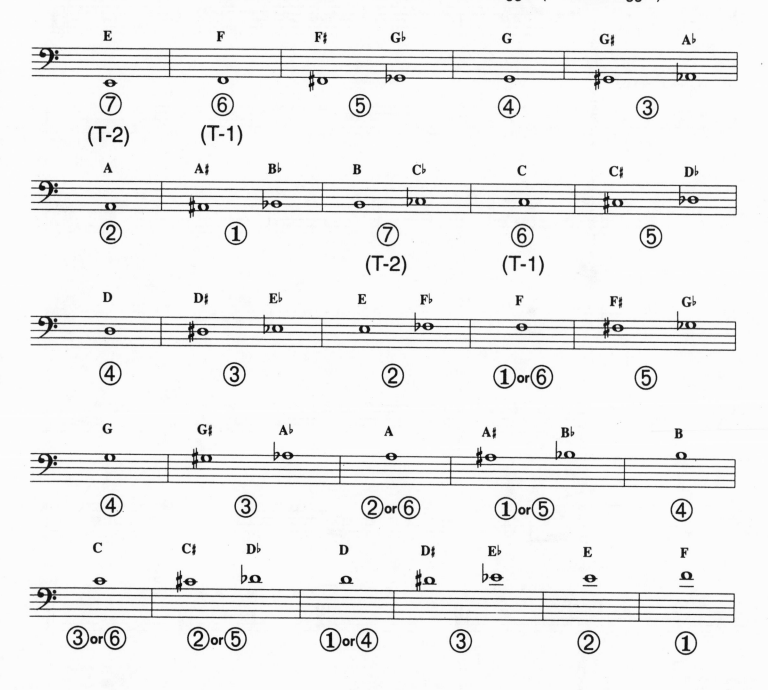